Original title:
Friends by Choice, Not by Chance

Copyright © 2024 Swan Charm
All rights reserved.

Author: Lan Donne
ISBN HARDBACK: 978-9916-86-860-7
ISBN PAPERBACK: 978-9916-86-861-4
ISBN EBOOK: 978-9916-86-862-1

## The Family We Choose

In laughter and joy, we find our place,
Bonded by love, we share warm grace.
Through thick and thin, we stand as one,
Together we shine, like the rising sun.

With open hearts, we navigate time,
Each story we weave, a shared rhyme.
We lift each other when shadows fall,
In unity's strength, we conquer all.

In moments of doubt, we find our way,
Hand in hand, we bravely sway.
Through trials faced, our spirits soar,
The family we choose, forever more.

With every cheer, we celebrate life,
In joy and in sorrow, through peace and strife.
Our laughter echoes, our memories thrive,
In this chosen bond, we truly arrive.

The ties that bind may not be of blood,
Yet deeper than roots, they grow like a flood.
In this canvas of love, we paint our view,
Together we're strong, the family we choose.

## Bonds Beyond Blood

In shadows deep, we found our way,
A friendship strong, come what may.
Through trials faced, we stand as one,
In hearts entwined, our battles won.

No ties of flesh, yet love runs deep,
In laughter shared, in secrets keep.
We weave the light, dispel the dark,
With every breath, we leave our mark.

In distant lands, or by the sea,
You are my home, you are my free.
Our stories dance, like waves that crest,
In bonds beyond, we are truly blessed.

## Embraced in Kindred Spirit

Two souls collide, in gentle embrace,
We share a fire, a sacred space.
With whispered dreams, we touch the stars,
In kindred spirit, there are no bars.

Your laughter rings, like sweet refrain,
A melody soft that eases pain.
Through every storm, we find our way,
With open hearts, we greet each day.

In silence shared, our spirits soar,
A bond unbroken, forevermore.
Together we stand, in joy and strife,
Embraced in spirit, the dance of life.

## The Tapestry of Trust

Thread by thread, we weave our tale,
In moments soft, when storms prevail.
Colors bright, in shades of care,
In the tapestry, our hearts laid bare.

A pattern rich, with love's embrace,
With every stitch, we find our place.
Through trials borne, together strong,
In trust, we find where we belong.

With each day's dawn, new threads align,
In silent vows, our lives entwine.
The fabric holds, through thick and thin,
In the tapestry of trust, we begin.

## Harmonizing in Unison

In harmony, our voices rise,
A symphony under open skies.
Each note a story, gently sung,
In unison, we're still so young.

With hearts attuned, we find our beat,
In melodies that make us complete.
Through highs and lows, our song remains,
In every joy, in every pain.

Together we dance, a timeless flow,
In the rhythm of life, we come to know.
With every chord, our spirits blend,
Harmonizing strong, as we transcend.

## Together We Rise

In shadows cast, we find the light,
With open hearts, we stand upright.
Hand in hand, we'll face the storm,
Together strong, in every form.

Through trials faced, we learn and grow,
In unity, our spirits flow.
Each whisper shared, a gentle guide,
In every heart, our dreams abide.

With every step, we share our fate,
In laughter's joy, we celebrate.
No mountain high, no valley low,
Together bound, we'll always glow.

As nights turn dark, we find our flame,
In every loss, we play the game.
With steadfast hope, we touch the skies,
In bonds of love, together we rise.

Through every tear, we heal the pain,
In every joy, we hope again.
With open arms, we soar so high,
In unity, together we fly.

## **Paths Converged**

Once upon a winding way,
Two souls met in bright array.
Destinies with threads entwined,
In shared moments, hearts aligned.

Through forests deep and valleys wide,
We journey forth, side by side.
With every step, the world unfolds,
In laughter's warmth, the future holds.

Each story shared, a fragrant bouquet,
In every word, we find our sway.
With trust and faith, we carve our mark,
In the tapestry, we leave a spark.

As seasons change and shadows fade,
In love's embrace, we're unafraid.
With every turn, new dreams arise,
Paths converged beneath the skies.

In every heartbeat, a song we sing,
With open arms, the joy we bring.
Together forged, forever strong,
In harmony, we all belong.

## The Alchemy of Affinity

In the cauldron of our minds,
Ideas mix, the heart unwinds.
With every touch, a new delight,
In shared moments, we ignite.

Through whispered dreams and silent sighs,
We sculpt our world, the spirit flies.
In the dance of chance, we find our way,
Creating gold from the light of day.

A tapestry of hopes and fears,
In laughter's echoes, we shed our tears.
With every glance, a secret shared,
In alchemy, our souls are bared.

As shadows linger, finding light,
In unity, we face the night.
With passion's flame, we rise and shine,
In this bond, our paths align.

Through every change, the magic flows,
In growth we bloom, in love we chose.
The alchemy of hearts set free,
In this connection, we will be.

## The Canvas of Companionship

On a canvas wide, we paint our dreams,
With colors bold, life's flowing streams.
In every stroke, our stories blend,
In this creation, love transcends.

With gentle brushes, we shape our days,
In laughter's hues, the heart conveys.
Each moment cherished, a work of art,
In this canvas, we play our part.

Through vibrant shades of joy and strife,
We navigate the colors of life.
In every line, a tale unfolds,
In the warmth of friendship, love beholds.

As seasons shift, our palette grows,
In every change, the spirit knows.
With open minds, we embrace the light,
In companionship, we take our flight.

On this canvas, we'll forever stay,
In vibrant hues, come what may.
Together in this journey vast,
The canvas of companionship holds fast.

## Connections of the Heart

In whispers soft, we share our dreams,
A bond unbroken, or so it seems,
Through trials faced and joys we find,
A tapestry woven, two souls entwined.

In laughter bright, our spirits soar,
Each fleeting glance unlocks a door,
The rhythm beats, a pulsing art,
In every moment, connections start.

Through storms we weather, hand in hand,
With silent strength, together we stand,
In shadows cast, our light will glow,
For in our hearts, we truly know.

The pages turn, the story grows,
In every heartbeat, love bestows,
A dance of years, both wild and free,
Through every chapter, you and me.

So lift your gaze, for love's embrace,
In every tear, in every grace,
These connections forged, forever true,
A symphony played, just me and you.

## The Garden We Cultivate

In sunlight's glow, our seeds are sown,
With careful hands, love's labor grown,
Each flower blooms with colors bright,
In this garden, we find our light.

Among the leaves, our laughter sings,
As nature hums of simple things,
We nurture roots, both strong and deep,
Where secrets whispered, dreams we keep.

In every weed, a lesson learned,
With patience held, and passions burned,
Our hopes arise like blossoms fair,
In fragrant air, we find our share.

Through rain that falls, through skies of gray,
We cultivate love, come what may,
With every dawn, new wonders greet,
In this garden, life is sweet.

So hand in hand, we tend the land,
With faith and trust, together we stand,
A love that thrives, a bond so true,
In this garden, it's me and you.

## **Companions by Design**

By fate's own hand, our paths aligned,
In every stride, a thread defined,
Together woven, we journey long,
In harmony found, where we belong.

With shared adventures, we paint the skies,
In every glance, a world of sighs,
A laughter echoes through the years,
With heartfelt joy and brimming tears.

As seasons change, our spirits grow,
In each embrace, the warmth will flow,
With gentle words, we heal each scar,
Companions close, no matter how far.

Through every storm, through sunlit days,
In whispered hopes and endless ways,
By design, we carve our fate,
With love as anchor, never too late.

So dance with me, through life's grand scheme,
Together chasing every dream,
Forever bound, our spirits will shine,
In this journey, you're forever mine.

# **Crafted Companionship**

In quiet spaces, our hearts entwine,
With every story, your soul meets mine,
A crafted bond, both strong and rare,
In each shared glance, we lay us bare.

Through trials faced, and laughter shared,
In moments tender, we are paired,
With every challenge, we grow wise,
As trust embraces, like morning skies.

In whispered dreams and softest sighs,
We learn to soar, we learn to rise,
With threads of hope that pull us near,
In every heartbeat, love draws near.

In shades of life, both dark and bright,
We find our way, guided by light,
Together crafting a tapestry,
In this companionship, you're part of me.

So let us weave through time and space,
In every moment, find our place,
With crafted hearts, we navigate,
In this journey, we celebrate.

## **Destined to Connect**

In the quiet of night we find,
Threads of fate that bind us tight.
Stars align in patterns designed,
Two souls spark with gentle light.

Waves of laughter, whispers shared,
In the warmth of friendship's glow.
Hearts entwined, we feel prepared,
For adventures yet to show.

Through the storms and sunny days,
Hand in hand, we'll face it all.
In the moments, love conveys,
A bond that never lets us fall.

With every challenge that we meet,
Together we will stand as one.
In this dance, we find our beat,
Our journey has only begun.

Whispers of a future bright,
Our paths forever interlace.
In the darkness, we are light,
Destined souls in time and space.

## **Crafted in Kindness**

A gentle hand extended wide,
In the corners of the heart.
Through our smiles, love is supplied,
Building bridges, never apart.

Small gestures weave a greater thread,
A tapestry of care we share.
In every word, our spirits spread,
Crafted kindness, everywhere.

In shared laughter, life unfolds,
With every moment, we create.
Stories of our hearts retold,
In kindness, we illuminate.

Together we shall face the storm,
With compassion as our guide.
In a world where love transforms,
Kindness stands ever by our side.

As we walk this precious lane,
Let our hearts be open-wide.
In the joy and in the pain,
Crafted kindness is our pride.

## Navigating Life Together

Hand in hand, we wander far,
Through the hills and valleys low.
Every journey, like a star,
Guides us through the ebb and flow.

With every twist, with every turn,
Lessons learned along the way.
In each moment, hearts will burn,
Together we embrace the day.

Maps may fade, but hearts align,
Trust the compass of our dreams.
In the unknown, our spirits shine,
Navigating life's wild streams.

Through the laughter, through the tears,
Every heartbeat, every sigh.
Together we will face our fears,
As we chase the boundless sky.

In this dance of give and take,
Creating paths with every step.
In the love, our souls awake,
Navigating life, our promise kept.

## Serendipitous Synchronicity

In moments where our paths collide,
Magic lingers in the air.
Unexpected joys, the heart's guide,
A dance of fate beyond compare.

The universe, it knows our names,
In whispers soft, it points the way.
Coincidences like gentle flames,
Igniting dreams both bright and gay.

As we wander through this life,
Unseen forces pull us near.
In the beauty and the strife,
Serendipity draws us clear.

With every turn we take in stride,
Gifts of fate unfold their grace.
In unity, we'll abide,
Finding joy in life's embrace.

So let us trust the unseen thread,
That weaves through time like silver lines.
In this tapestry we've read,
Serendipitous synchronicity shines.

## Our Shared Adventure

In the dawn of our shared dream,
We set forth on paths unseen.
Hand in hand, with gentle grace,
Together we embrace this space.

Mountains high and rivers wide,
With every step, you're by my side.
Through laughter and the rain we roam,
In each moment, we find our home.

Stars above guide our way,
In the night, our spirits sway.
With every heartbeat, we ignite,
A journey woven, pure delight.

Winding roads and turning tides,
In the treasure of time, truth hides.
With open hearts, we seek to find,
The stories that forever bind.

In the sunset's golden glow,
Together in the afterflow,
With memories etched, we stand tall,
In this adventure, we have it all.

## **Intentional Bonds**

In the stillness, we connect,
With words unspoken, hearts reflect.
The ties we share, a sacred thread,
In every moment, love is spread.

Through laughter echoing through the air,
Intentions weave us with gentle care.
Hand in hand in storms and sun,
With these bonds, we are as one.

Each glance a promise, soft and true,
In every silence, I see you.
Unraveling fears, we dare to trust,
In the foundation, love is a must.

Through trials faced, we find our way,
In each other, we choose to stay.
With every heartbeat, we transform,
Creating shelter amidst the storm.

In the garden of hearts we'll grow,
With roots entwined deep below.
In intentional love's warm embrace,
We dance through life, a sacred space.

## Pathways of the Heart

Upon the pathways where we tread,
With every step, new dreams are fed.
In the whispers of the trees,
Our hearts align, a gentle breeze.

Echoes of laughter fill the air,
In moments paused, we lay our care.
With every sunrise, hope unfolds,
A tapestry of love retold.

Through winding trails, we seek, we find,
In the shadows, our light is blind.
With open arms, we greet the day,
Together we shall pave the way.

In the tapestry of time, we weave,
The moments cherished, hearts believe.
With every heartbeat, love resounds,
On this journey, joy abounds.

In the fading light, we'll share our dreams,
With whispered wishes, soft moonbeams.
On pathways crafted just for us,
In this wandering, we place our trust.

## **Chosen to Walk Together**

In the quiet dawn, we find our way,
With hearts aligned, come what may.
Each moment shared, a treasure deep,
In the bond of love, we safely keep.

Through shadows cast, our laughter bright,
In every challenge, we take flight.
Hand in hand, our spirits soar,
Together, we unlock each door.

With gentle words, we calm the storm,
In warmth of love, we feel the charm.
In the glow of the moon, we reflect,
On the path ahead, we feel respect.

Through winding roads and choices wide,
In the journey, we choose our stride.
With every heartbeat, strength we find,
In this union, beautifully entwined.

In the tapestry of life we weave,
With threads of hope, we dare believe.
Forever chosen, side by side,
In this journey, we shall abide.

## **Moonlit Connections**

In the quiet night, we gaze,
Under silver beams, we blaze,
Whispers in the warm, soft light,
Hearts entwined in sheer delight.

Stars above like dreams so bright,
Guide our souls through velvet night,
In this dance, we find our way,
Moonlit paths where shadows play.

Every glance feels like a spark,
Lighting up the world so dark,
In your eyes, the universe,
A love story, none could curse.

Waves of calm flow through the air,
Holding tight, without a care,
In this moment, we are free,
Moonlit whispers call to me.

Together we ride the tide,
With you always by my side,
In the glow, our spirits soar,
Connected now, forevermore.

## **Companions in the Dance**

In the swirl of spirits bright,
We twirl beneath the starry night,
Every step, a heartbeat shared,
In this moment, we are dared.

Hands connect as music flows,
To the rhythm, love still grows,
Laughter tunes our every turn,
In your warmth, my heart will burn.

Shadows play upon the floor,
With each movement, we explore,
Hearts aligned in perfect grace,
In your arms, I find my place.

Faces close, the world fades out,
In this dance, there is no doubt,
Together, we will brave the night,
Two companions holding tight.

As the stars above collide,
In this dance, our souls confide,
With each spin, our spirits rise,
Bound forever, no goodbyes.

## Gossamer Threads of Choice

In the weave of life's design,
Threads of hope and fate align,
Choices made with utmost care,
Moments shimmer in the air.

Every path holds chance and change,
In the fabric, we arrange,
Colors bright, and shadows deep,
Promises that we must keep.

Gossamer strands, light and fine,
Guide us on through space and time,
Each decision, a gentle pull,
Woven dreams that feel so full.

With each step on this fine thread,
Every whisper, kindness said,
In this tapestry we trust,
Strength in bonds of gold and rust.

In the quiet, voices sound,
Echoes of our hearts abound,
Gossamer threads, we shall embrace,
In our choices, find our place.

## **Unbreakable Ties**

In the silence, bonds resonate,
Unbreakable ties that shape our fate,
Through the storms and gentle days,
Together still, our spirits blaze.

Across the miles, our hearts remain,
Bound by joy, or shared pain,
In every laugh, in every tear,
An unspoken truth draws near.

Embers glow, a lasting fire,
Roots that dig through deep desire,
Though the winds may shift and change,
Our connection will never drain.

Life may throw its curves and bends,
But love's thread never ends,
In the tapestry of time,
Our story weaves, forever prime.

Through the years, we will stand tall,
Answering each other's call,
Unbreakable, our spirits fly,
Hand in hand, we touch the sky.

## United by Choice

In a world that spins so fast,
We choose to hold on tight,
Through laughter and through tears,
Together, we find light.

Our paths have crossed with grace,
Two hearts beating as one,
Through every challenge faced,
We've only just begun.

The road may twist and turn,
Yet hand in hand we'll go,
With every bridge we burn,
Stronger love will grow.

In whispers soft and clear,
Our voices intertwine,
With every hope and fear,
Our spirits brightly shine.

United by our choice,
We forge our destiny,
In every shared rejoice,
We are forever free.

## The Symphony of Affection

A gentle breeze does play,
With notes so sweet and pure,
Each moment, night and day,
A love that will endure.

In every glance, a spark,
In laughter, melodies,
A symphony, not stark,
Composed with heart's degrees.

With every heartbeat's thrum,
We dance in perfect time,
Creating waves of hum,
A timeless, rhyming climb.

When silence fills the air,
Our souls still softly sing,
In harmony we share,
The joy that love can bring.

This symphony we've made,
Resonates within us,
A masterpiece displayed,
In love, we place our trust.

## Nurtured by Trust

In the garden of our hearts,
Where tender feelings grow,
Each secret, like fine arts,
In sunlight's warmest glow.

With roots that intertwine,
We cultivate our dreams,
In fertile ground, we shine,
Flowing with life's sweet streams.

To nurture is to care,
To feed what makes us whole,
With patience we will share,
The harvest of our soul.

Through doubts that come and go,
We water with our trust,
In storms, our love will flow,
A bond that's truly just.

Each flourish is a sign,
That love, it knows no bounds,
In unity, we find,
The strength that love surrounds.

## **Anchors in the Storm**

When waves of doubt arise,
And tempests test our plea,
We find the strength to rise,
Together, you and me.

With storms that twist and churn,
And skies that bleed with gray,
Our hearts, they softly yearn,
For calm in disarray.

In chaos, we will stand,
As anchors, firm and strong,
Through roughest seas, we've planned,
In unity belong.

With every thunder's clap,
We hold each other tight,
In love, we find our map,
A beacon in the night.

We'll weather every gale,
For love will see us through,
Together we prevail,
In storms, we are the true.

## **Chosen Kinship**

In a garden where we grow,
Roots intertwine, love in tow.
Every smile, a radiant sun,
Together we shine, forever one.

Through the storms we find our way,
Hand in hand, come what may.
With each story, hearts align,
In this bond, our lives entwine.

In laughter's echo, we reside,
Side by side, we take the ride.
Through every joy, through every tear,
Chosen kin, forever near.

As seasons change, we start anew,
In every shade, our friendship grew.
Through winding paths, we dare to roam,
In each other, we find home.

With every challenge we embrace,
We find strength in love's warm grace.
In the quiet, in the song,
Together we know where we belong.

## **Threads of Choice**

In the tapestry of fate,
We weave our dreams, create our state.
Every choice, a vibrant thread,
In this fabric, hope is spread.

With hands entwined, we stitch the dawn,
In our hearts, a love reborn.
Through myriad paths, we navigate,
Together strong, we elevate.

With every whisper, a tale unfolds,
Secrets kept, and courage bold.
In every tear, in every laugh,
We find the joy, the perfect draft.

In shadows deep, we find the light,
Guiding each other through the night.
With every bond, we navigate,
The choices made, our fates await.

Through vibrant hues, our journey flows,
In the garden where friendship grows.
Every step, a dance of grace,
Threads of choice that time won't erase.

## Companions in the Mist

In the morning's gentle haze,
We wander through life's winding ways.
With whispered dreams, we take the chance,
In the mist, we find our dance.

Every footstep, a story shared,
In silence strong, we have dared.
Through the fog, our laughter rings,
Together we face what the daylight brings.

Through the shadows of the past,
We forge a bond that's built to last.
In the twilight, we chase the dawn,
Companions true, we carry on.

In the quiet, our hearts align,
With every moment, love will shine.
In the misty veil, we find our sight,
Together we embrace the light.

With every heartbeat, we're entwined,
In the mystery, our dreams defined.
As companions, we rise and soar,
In the mist, we seek for more.

## **The Art of Togetherness**

In a canvas brushed with care,
We paint our lives, a dream to share.
With every stroke, our colors blend,
In this art, there's no end.

Through thick and thin, we find our way,
In harmony, we choose to stay.
With gentle hands, we build the frame,
In togetherness, we stake our claim.

In whispered thoughts, our hearts converse,
With every moment, we immerse.
Through laughter bright, through tears that fall,
Together we conquer, together we call.

With every season, a brush of change,
In the spectrum, we rearrange.
The art of love, a masterpiece,
In each other, we find release.

In the gallery of our dreams,
In every glance, the magic beams.
Through the journey, we'll paint our song,
In the art of togetherness, we belong.

## Souls Affined

In shadows deep, our spirits dance,
United grace in every glance.
A whispered bond, so pure and strong,
In perfect tune, we both belong.

Across the stars, our paths entwine,
A sacred thread, a love divine.
Though tempest wild may blow and roar,
Our hearts ignite, forevermore.

In silent nights, when dreams take flight,
We find our way, bathed in moonlight.
Hand in hand, we roam the skies,
With every breath, a sweet surprise.

Through time and space, we weave a tale,
Of love that's bright, that will not pale.
An endless journey, near or far,
Together still, just as we are.

With spirits linked, we dare to trust,
In every moment, love is a must.
Through life's embrace, we shall explore,
Two souls as one, forevermore.

## **Alliances of the Heart**

In quiet corners of the day,
Our laughter joins in joyous play.
Two hearts that beat in sweet refrain,
A harmony that ebbs, and gains.

Through trials faced, we stand as one,
With hands that hold, and dreams begun.
In whispered words and secret signs,
Our love a tapestry, that shines.

With every glance, a promise made,
In storms of life, we won't evade.
Together strong, through thick and thin,
An alliance forged, we both shall win.

In moments brief, or years at stake,
A bond much deeper than just fate.
Through all the seasons, high or low,
Our hearts remain a steady glow.

So here's to love, our guiding light,
In darkness deep, it's shining bright.
With every step, together we go,
Alliances of hearts will ever grow.

## Companions from the Stars

Beneath the vast, celestial dome,
We find our way, we call it home.
With constellations as our guide,
Companions true, we shall not hide.

In cosmic winds, our spirits soar,
Through galaxies, we roam and explore.
With every flicker of a light,
Our dreams are woven through the night.

In stardust whispers, secrets shared,
The universe knows how much we cared.
Through time and space, we'll navigate,
Together here, it's never too late.

We dance on rings of Saturn's grace,
With every turn, we find our place.
In nebula's glow, we carve our name,
A journey vast, but never plain.

So let us shine, like stars aligned,
Through cosmic paths, our hearts combined.
Together we'll find our secret Mars,
In the embrace of all the stars.

## Together by Intent

With every step, our purpose clear,
Structured dreams we build each year.
In unity, we find our might,
Together by intent, we ignite.

Through trials faced, we rise and soar,
In every heartbeat, we want more.
With visions bright and minds combined,
Our journey rich, our fates entwined.

In laughter shared and tears concealed,
The strength we have has been revealed.
With open hearts, our wishes blend,
In this vast world, we will transcend.

Through all the storms, we hold the line,
United in this love so fine.
A bond that time cannot unravel,
Together, we'll traverse this travel.

So here we stand, with hands embraced,
In every moment, love interlaced.
Together by intent, we'll strive,
With hearts so full, we'll always thrive.

## Navigating Together by Will

In a boat on seas we glide,
With sturdy oars, we row inside.
Together through the waves we weave,
With trust in hearts, we dare believe.

The stars above our guiding light,
With every breath, we face the night.
A journey shared, a course so true,
In unity we find what's new.

The winds may shift and paths may change,
But with our strength, we rearrange.
With courage as a shared refrain,
Through stormy weather, we remain.

A compass crafted from our dreams,
With kindred spirits, nothing seems.
The world is vast, yet we explore,
In this adventure, we implore.

So hand in hand, we steer ahead,
With hope and love, our spirits fed.
Together navigating life,
Through joy and pain, through calm and strife.

## **The Ties We Forge**

In silent moments, bonds are made,
With whispered dreams that never fade.
Through laughter shared and tears we shed,
The ties we forge, they gently spread.

Like branches strong on ancient trees,
With roots that twist in gentle breeze.
A network lived, a dance of fate,
In every heartbeat, we create.

Through trials faced, we stand as one,
A tapestry of life begun.
With colors bright, our stories meld,
In every thread, our dreams upheld.

Connection deepens, spirits rise,
In every glance, the truth belies.
We hold each other, fierce and free,
The ties we forge, our legacy.

So gather close, let's weave anew,
In every moment, strength imbue.
Together we can face the world,
With every heart, our love unfurled.

## Hearts Entwined in Purpose

With every step, our paths align,
In shared pursuits, our souls entwine.
Through challenges, we share the load,
Hearts intertwined, we walk the road.

A vision clear that lights our way,
With purpose strong, we seize the day.
Together we can climb the heights,
In unity, we spark the lights.

Our voices join, a sweet refrain,
A harmony that breaks the chain.
Through dreams pursued and passions found,
In every heartbeat, love surrounds.

With hope as ours, we build our fate,
In every moment, never late.
Through trials faced, we rise anew,
With hearts entwined, we push on through.

So let us soar on wings of grace,
In every challenge, find our place.
Together we can touch the skies,
With purpose true, our spirits rise.

## Crafted Confidants

In whispered secrets, trust is born,
With laughter shared from dusk till morn.
Through every story, moments shared,
Crafted confidants, fully bared.

With open hearts, we share our woes,
In gentle ways, our garden grows.
The roots run deep, the bonds we tend,
In every sorrow, love extends.

Through breaking dawns and dusk's embrace,
We find in each a sacred space.
With laughter ringing through the air,
Crafted confidants, a treasure rare.

The world may change, but we stay true,
In every challenge, me and you.
With every moment, grace be sought,
Together facing what life's brought.

So let's recount the tales we've spun,
In every battle fought and won.
For in this friendship, gold we find,
Crafted confidants, hearts entwined.

## Whispers of the Heart

In quiet corners of the night,
Soft murmurs play, a gentle light.
Carried softly on the breeze,
They weave through dreams like swaying trees.

Words unspoken find their way,
In tender glances, hopes will stay.
A connection deep, though rarely seen,
In the silence lies what could have been.

Echoes linger, hearts feel near,
Fear melts away when love is clear.
Each heartbeat sings a sacred tune,
In whispers shared, beneath the moon.

Secrets held in shadows sway,
Guiding souls that drift astray.
With every sigh, new paths unfold,
In whispers, we find stories told.

So let the murmurs fill the air,
With every breath, we learn to care.
In the stillness, love will chart,
The timeless dance of every heart.

## **Bonds Forged in Time**

In golden rays of morning light,
We build our dreams, our futures bright.
Each moment shared, a thread anew,
Woven strong, with trust and true.

Through trials faced, we stand as one,
A tapestry of battles won.
In laughter shared and tears we shed,
Our hearts entwined, no words unsaid.

Seasons change, yet still we stay,
Through winding paths, we find our way.
In quiet strength, in joy and strife,
The bond we share gives meaning to life.

Memories crafted, like fine art,
Each chapter penned, more than a part.
In every glance, the years align,
A journey marked by love divine.

And as the stars begin to shine,
We celebrate what's yours and mine.
Forever linked, through space and time,
In cherished moments, our hearts chime.

# The Magic of Connection

Two souls collide, a spark ignites,
In whispered dreams and starry nights.
A glance exchanged, a knowing smile,
In those small moments, love's first trial.

The universe conspires to share,
A magic felt, a vibrant air.
In every touch, a story flows,
In every heartbeat, truth bestows.

Through laughter, tears, both highs and lows,
A garden blooms, love only grows.
Intertwined, as roots embrace,
In this connection, we find our place.

Time may pass, but still we hold,
A bond that's warm, that breaks the cold.
In harmony, we dance and sway,
Together, come what may, we'll stay.

So let the magic guide our way,
In every moment, night and day.
With open hearts, let dreams take flight,
In this connection, all feels right.

## **Stepping Stones of Intent**

Upon the path where dreams reside,
We lay our stones, with hearts as guide.
Each step we take, with purpose strong,
In silent oaths, we sing our song.

Intentions clear, like morning dew,
Illuminate the path we pursue.
With every choice, the journey starts,
Guided by the whispers of our hearts.

Through twists and turns, the journey flows,
With each new stone, the courage grows.
Though shadows linger, light breaks through,
With faith as compass, we push on anew.

In moments shared, in laughter light,
Each stone we place, a new delight.
Together, building what's to be,
A future bright, for you and me.

As footprints mark the way we tread,
With love and hope, the path is spread.
Each step a promise, every bend,
In stepping stones, our journey blends.

## Authentic Chosen Paths

In whispers soft, the choices call,
We walk our roads, both short and tall.
Each step we take, a story spun,
In shadows cast, the light we've won.

Through tangled woods, we seek our fate,
With open hearts, we navigate.
The paths we forge, no map in hand,
Are painted bright, in dreams we stand.

A traveler's soul knows not of fear,
For every trail, the stars are near.
The journey calls, a sweet embrace,
In every turn, we find our place.

From mountain peaks to ocean's edge,
We hold our truth, we make our pledge.
With every stride, we find our way,
In choices made, we shape our day.

Each path is ours, uniquely drawn,
In quiet strength, we greet the dawn.
With love as light, we boldly go,
In chosen paths, our spirits grow.

**Mosaics of Memory**

Fragments shine, in colors bright,
A tapestry of day and night.
Each piece a tale, a life well-lived,
In whispered dreams, our hearts are sieved.

The laughter shared, the tears we weep,
In every moment, memories deep.
A mosaic formed of joy and pain,
In every loss, there's love to gain.

The echoes ring of days gone by,
In twilight's glow, we laugh, we sigh.
With every stitch, our stories weave,
In woven time, we dare believe.

Old photographs in dusty frames,
Capture smiles, and whisper names.
In memories held, we find our ground,
In cherished moments, joy is found.

Together we live, each tale unfolds,
In gentle glances, our truth beholds.
The past a gift, the future bright,
In mosaics of memory, we find our light.

## **Allies in the Dance of Life**

With open hearts, we take the floor,
In harmony, we seek for more.
Each step a bond, in rhythm's beat,
Together we rise, together we meet.

In swirling grace, our spirits blend,
Through trials faced, we learn to mend.
A dance of trust, a circle wide,
In every leap, we find our pride.

The music flows, a vibrant sound,
In every twirl, our hope is found.
With every glance, a silent vow,
In every moment, here and now.

As partners strong, we lift each other,
In this great dance, we are like no other.
Through gentle turns, and spins anew,
In life's embrace, we will break through.

Together we stand, side by side,
In the dance of life, we won't divide.
With every breath, we weave our song,
In the joy of dance, we all belong.

## **Unscripted Connections**

In chance encounters, magic blooms,
In simple moments, friendship looms.
With every smile, our paths align,
In unscripted ways, our souls entwine.

Beneath the stars, our stories meet,
In whispered words, our hearts repeat.
A fleeting glance, a knowing spark,
In every bond, we ignite the dark.

With open arms, we learn to share,
Through laughter bright, we show we care.
Each heartbeat drumming to life's sweet tune,
In uncharted skies, we find our rune.

The world a stage, with roles unplanned,
In serendipity, together we stand.
With every twist, our lives connect,
In threads unseen, a love perfect.

In moments pure, we find our peace,
In every glance, the worries cease.
With open hearts, we choose to grow,
In unscripted paths, our spirits flow.

## Our Chosen Adventure

We set our sights on the distant shore,
With dreams that whisper and spirits that soar.
Through fields of gold and skies of blue,
Hand in hand, we'll find our view.

The roads may twist and the winds might howl,
But together we'll laugh, we'll sing, we'll prowl.
Each moment a treasure, each step a delight,
In this chosen adventure, our hearts take flight.

From mountain peaks to valleys low,
With every sunrise, new wonders grow.
The map is drawn by the love we share,
Guided by trust, we journey with care.

Through stormy nights and sunny days,
We wander forth, lost in a haze.
But in each other, we find our way,
In our chosen adventure, come what may.

So here's to the moments that make us whole,
With laughter and tears that nourish the soul.
For every path taken, we brave and explore,
In this chosen adventure, we cherish and soar.

## Cherished Paths

In the quiet of dusk, where shadows play,
We walk on paths that gently sway.
Each step we take is a story to tell,
In cherished paths, we both dwell.

The leaves rustle softly, the stars start to blink,
With every whisper, our hearts start to sync.
Together we wander, as time slips away,
On these cherished paths, forever we sway.

Through fragrant meadows and forests deep,
In moments of silence, in laughter we leap.
Hand in hand, we're never apart,
Each cherished path leads to the heart.

The journey is long, but hope is our guide,
With memories made, and love by our side.
In every turn, there's a magic to find,
On these cherished paths, our souls intertwined.

So let us tread softly, with joy in our stride,
For each cherished path is a source of pride.
In the book of our lives, these pages will last,
As we walk together on cherished paths.

## The Ties We Nurture

In whispers of love, our bond begins,
A gentle embrace, where trust never thins.
Through storms we weather, and skies that gleam,
The ties we nurture hold strong as a dream.

With laughter that dances and tears that flow,
In every heartbeat, our emotions grow.
United we stand, in shadows and light,
The ties we nurture make everything right.

Each story shared, a treasure unveiled,
Through trials faced, our faith prevailed.
In the depth of silence, or in joyous cheer,
The ties we nurture forever hold dear.

As seasons change, and years swiftly pass,
With memories woven like blades of grass.
In every moment, our spirits ignite,
The ties we nurture, a beacon so bright.

So here's to the love that we lovingly weave,
In the tapestry of life, we truly believe.
For the ties we nurture, no distance can sever,
Bound by our hearts, we're united forever.

## **Bonded by Hearts**

In the quiet of night, we find our way,
With whispers of love that gently sway.
Two souls entwined, under the moon's glow,
Bonded by hearts, through time we flow.

Through laughter and tears, we stand side by side,
In the warmth of our bond, there's nothing to hide.
With dreams interlaced, and hopes held high,
Bonded by hearts, together we fly.

The journey is ours, through thick and through thin,
In moments of weakness, we share strength within.
With every heartbeat, we cherish the start,
For we are forever, bonded by heart.

In the light of the sun and the starry night,
We draw from our love, an endless delight.
No distance too great, no challenge too hard,
With love as our compass, we'll never discard.

So here's to the bond that forever will last,
With memories made, and shadows cast.
For in this life, through every depart,
We find our way home, bonded by heart.

## The Art of Togetherness

In quiet corners, laughter grows,
Hands entwined where love bestows,
In the dance of light and shade,
Together, dreams are gently laid.

Voices blend in sweet refrain,
Through the joy, through the pain,
Colors mingle, hearts collide,
In unity, we choose to bide.

Moments shared, a sacred art,
Every echo, every part,
In the stillness of the night,
Together we find our light.

Building bridges, not just walls,
In the silence, love still calls,
Hand in hand, we forge our way,
Through the night, into the day.

Together, we are not alone,
In the heart, a steadfast home,
Every challenge, side by side,
In the journey, we abide.

## Together We Rise

With every dawn, we chase the sun,
Together we stand, we are not one,
In strength we find our shared embrace,
In every heartbeat, we leave a trace.

When shadows fall, we hold the light,
With dreams ignited, taking flight,
Through storms that roar and winds that chime,
Together we craft our rhythm and rhyme.

Our voices rise, a chorus clear,
In harmony, we conquer fear,
The chains of doubt we will unbind,
In unity, true peace we find.

Through trials thick and battles long,
The bond of love shall keep us strong,
Together we thrive, together we dare,
In the depth of care, we find our prayer.

So hand in hand, let's forge ahead,
In the tapestry of life, we're wed,
With hope as our guiding star,
Together we rise, no matter how far.

# Handpicked Hearts

In a garden where friendships bloom,
Handpicked hearts dispel all gloom,
With tender care, we plant the seeds,
In shared laughter, love proceeds.

Each moment cherished, rare and bright,
In every hug, we find our light,
Through seasons change, the roots will grow,
Handpicked hearts, a gentle flow.

We gather strength, in joy we bask,
In simple truths, it's love we ask,
Through whispered dreams, the world we share,
Handpicked hearts, beyond compare.

In the tapestry of days gone by,
Together we'll reach for the sky,
For every heart, a story told,
Handpicked warmth, a love to hold.

As time unfolds, we shall remain,
In every joy and every pain,
With handpicked hearts, we'll face the test,
In unity, we are truly blessed.

## A Symphony of Souls

In the silence, a note is born,
A melody for hearts to adorn,
With every breath, the music flows,
A symphony only love knows.

In harmony, our spirits soar,
With every rhythm, we explore,
The dance of life, both sweet and grand,
A symphony, hand in hand.

Each voice a thread in the grand design,
Together we sparkle, together we shine,
Through varied tones, a story plays,
A symphony that forever stays.

In the quiet, the whispers ring,
Through every struggle, we shall sing,
With courage bold, we write the score,
In unity, we'll seek for more.

The final note, a soft embrace,
In every soul, there's a sacred space,
Together we weave our endless whole,
In the heart's rhythm, a symphony of souls.

## Connections Built on Will

In quiet moments, hands entwined,
A bond forged in the fire of intent.
We build our dreams, hearts aligned,
With every choice, a new ascent.

Through trials faced, together we stand,
Our voices strong, a harmonious blend.
With each small step, we understand,
That love is the journey, not just the end.

In laughter shared, in silence embraced,
We weave a tapestry, rich and bright.
With every challenge, our spirits faced,
Each thread a testament, through day and night.

Beyond the noise, we find our way,
In whispered vows, our spirits soar.
Through every storm and bright array,
Connections built on will, we explore.

## Beyond the Tides of Time

Waves whisper secrets from times unknown,
They carry stories on the breeze.
Each crest a memory, each fall a tone,
In the ebb of life, we find our peace.

Stars above shine with ancient light,
Guiding us through night's embrace.
In their glow, our futures ignite,
As we dance through the cosmic space.

Moments linger like grains of sand,
Slipping through fingers, yet ever near.
In every heartbeat, a timeless strand,
Binding the past, present, and sphere.

With every tide, we learn to grow,
To navigate life's vast, open sea.
Beyond the tides, our spirits flow,
In unity, we set ourselves free.

## Kin of the Heart

In shared glances, a silent pact,
Our souls weave stories, old and new.
Through laughter and tears, a sacred act,
In this circle, our hearts renew.

Together we gather, under the sun,
Each tale a thread in our common quilt.
With every heartbeat, our lives are spun,
A fabric of memories, love distilled.

Through trials faced, we stand as one,
In shadows deep, we light the way.
With every dawn, a new day begun,
Our kinship shines, come what may.

In moments cherished, bonds we create,
With joy and strength, we nurture and mend.
Through every season, our love won't wait,
For in our hearts, we find a friend.

## Chosen Paths

On winding roads, with steps so bold,
We carve our fates beneath the skies.
With dreams unfurled, our stories told,
Each choice a star that brightly flies.

In shadowed woods and sunlit glades,
We wander through the mystery.
Each twist and turn, a dance cascades,
In the heart of life's grand tapestry.

Hand in hand, we face unknown,
With courage sewn into our seams.
Through trials met, and seeds we've sown,
Together we nurture our shared dreams.

With every path that we embrace,
A symphony of life's sweet breath.
In chosen ways, we find our place,
In love we flourish, defying death.

## The Light of Intentionality

In shadows deep where thoughts reside,
A spark ignites, a flame inside.
With careful steps, we find our way,
Intentional hearts guide the day.

We strive to grow, to understand,
To build a world with mindful hands.
In every choice, a chance to shine,
The light of love, a path divine.

Through whispers soft, our spirits soar,
With open hearts, we seek for more.
In unity, we rise as one,
Intentional lives, brightly spun.

The journey calls, with lessons vast,
With every moment, hold it fast.
The light within forever gleams,
Enkindled dreams weave vibrant streams.

Together bound, we forge ahead,
For every word and thought we've said.
In intentionality, we stand,
With love and purpose, hand in hand.

## **Weaving Lifelines**

In the loom of life, we find our thread,
One strand of hope, where dreams are fed.
With each connection, colors blend,
To form the lifelines we can send.

Through laughter shared and tears we sow,
We interlace the highs and lows.
With gentle care, the fibers twine,
Creating bonds that brightly shine.

In every story, a tapestry,
With threads of love running free.
Together woven, hearts embrace,
In unity, we find our place.

As seasons change, the patterns grow,
With every challenge, skills bestow.
Resilient ties in storms will stand,
Our woven lifelines, ever grand.

From dusk till dawn, the weavings show,
The courage found when we bestow.
With every stitch, we will define,
The bonds of friendship, pure and fine.

## **Threads of Intent**

Through life's vast fabric, threads we pull,
Each path we take, intentional.
In silence whisper, in actions bold,
The stories of the heart unfold.

With every choice, a thread we weave,
In hopes and dreams, we dare believe.
The patterns formed beneath our hands,
As life creates, together stands.

Sewn with purpose, visions clear,
In every heartbeat, we draw near.
With threads of intent, we shape our fate,
Creating beauty, never late.

Embracing love, we'll spin anew,
With colors bright, in every hue.
In grand designs, our spirits rise,
Threads of intent, our sacred ties.

Beyond the fabric, deeper still,
The essence of our heart's true will.
In unity, we'll thread the way,
With strength and grace, come what may.

## Crafted Companionship

In the hands of time, we sculpt our fate,
With crafted care, our hearts create.
Together journey, side by side,
In companionship, our hopes abide.

With laughter shared and tales we tell,
In memories cherished, we dwell.
Each moment seized, an artwork rare,
With crafted bonds beyond compare.

Through trials faced, our spirits rise,
In crafted strength, we touch the skies.
With every step, a vow we make,
In the warmth of love, we never break.

Life's intricate weave binds us tight,
In crafted companionship, pure delight.
Together bright, we light the dark,
In every heartbeat, there's a spark.

So let us flourish, hand in hand,
In crafted journeys across the land.
With love and trust, we'll always thrive,
Together in this dance, alive.

## Together on Purpose

In the quiet dawn, we rise,
Voices mingle in soft sighs.
Hand in hand, we find our way,
Guided by the light of day.

Through the storms, we will stand,
With unwavering hearts, so grand.
Each goal shared, a path we trace,
Together, we embrace our place.

Dreams entwined like rivers flow,
Growing stronger, we will grow.
With each step, the world we change,
United spirits, nothing strange.

And when shadows start to creep,
In each other's arms, we leap.
Trust and hope, our steadfast guide,
Forever walking side by side.

So here's to love, our endless drive,
With open hearts, we come alive.
Together we can face the night,
Illuminated by our light.

## The Mosaic of Affection

Countless pieces, all unique,
Each a story, silent speak.
Gathered here in vibrant hues,
We create the life we choose.

Laughter dances in the air,
Soft connections, so we care.
In the warmth of shared delight,
We weave our dreams, hold them tight.

Moments passed like gentle rain,
Washing thoughts of worry, pain.
Every smile, a stroke of light,
Painting futures, shining bright.

In this mosaic, hearts align,
All our colors intertwine.
With each piece, a bond we sprout,
Celebrating love throughout.

So here we stand, a canvas made,
In the love and joy conveyed.
With every touch, we break the night,
Creating art in purest light.

## Beautifully Aligned

Stars above, they shine so clear,
In their glow, we draw near.
Hearts in sync, a timeless dance,
Together we seize every chance.

Paths converged, like rivers flow,
In this journey, love will grow.
Aligned with dreams, we sail the seas,
In moments sweet, we find our ease.

With open eyes, we see the signs,
Faith and trust, our hearts entwined.
Through every trial, hand in hand,
From shadows cast, together we stand.

In the quiet of the night,
Whispers shared, hold us tight.
Every beat, a promise made,
Together, foundations laid.

So here we are, perfectly placed,
With every moment, love embraced.
Beautifully aligned, we shine,
Two souls dancing, yours and mine.

## **Lives Intertwined**

Fates entangled, like vines that climb,
In the garden rich with time.
Harvested dreams in gentle hands,
Together we'll create new lands.

Shared laughter beneath the sky,
Every tear, a reason why.
Through the seasons, strong we stand,
Love's warm glow, a guiding hand.

Paths may twist, yet we remain,
Navigating joy and pain.
In the tapestry we weave,
Threads of hope that never leave.

In the quiet, we find our voice,
In the chaos, we rejoice.
Lives intertwined, a sacred vow,
In this moment, here and now.

So take my hand, let's stroll ahead,
With every step, new dreams are fed.
Together, we will find our way,
In love's embrace, come what may.

## The Bonds We Choose

In whispered moments, we find our way,
A quiet strength that guides our play.
Through laughter shared and tears we shed,
These bonds we weave will never be dead.

With open hearts and hands held tight,
We stand as one through darkest night.
Each choice we make, a step we take,
In unity, our souls awake.

Together we rise, together we fall,
In this tapestry, we embrace it all.
The ties we form, both strong and true,
Are the sacred roots of me and you.

Through storms that rage and winds that blow,
Our chosen paths in love will grow.
In every smile, in every glance,
We celebrate this timeless dance.

So here we stand, hand in hand,
Together we build, together we stand.
In the garden of life, we nurture our choice,
In every heartbeat, we find our voice.

## **Threads of the Heart**

In every heartbeat, a story we weave,
Threads of affection, we choose to believe.
Colors collide in a vibrant array,
Together we flourish, come what may.

With laughter like sunlight, we light the way,
Binding us closer, day by day.
Through trials and triumphs, we stand so bold,
These threads of the heart are precious as gold.

Intertwined dreams, we dare to chase,
In this sacred bond, we find our place.
With eyes wide open, we see the art,
Stitched together, two worlds, one heart.

Through silence shared and stories swapped,
Our bonds grow deeper, never stopped.
In the fabric of life, we'll always be
Forever connected, you and me.

So let's embrace this beautiful thread,
In the journey of love, let's dare to tread.
Each knot we tie, a promise anew,
Threads of the heart, forever true.

## Chosen Souls Unite

In a world so vast, we found our place,
Two wandering souls, a fateful embrace.
With a spark igniting the night's dark sky,
Together we soar, learning to fly.

In moments of stillness, we share our fears,
A blend of laughter and salty tears.
With open hearts, we meet life's call,
Chosen souls unite, we rise, we fall.

Through paths uncharted, we pave our way,
Every step forward, a grand display.
Hand in hand, we face what's ahead,
In love's sweet dance, we are truly led.

With whispers of hope and dreams held tight,
We navigate shadows and embrace the light.
With every heartbeat, the promise resounds,
In our unity, love knows no bounds.

So here's to the journey, both yours and mine,
A tapestry woven, intricately fine.
Together we stand, forever in flight,
Chosen souls unite, our spirits ignite.

## Kinship Beyond Coincidence

In the thread of fate, we find our kin,
An unspoken bond, where love begins.
Through storms we weather, hand in hand,
A connection deeper than we planned.

Each laugh we share, a spark divine,
In life's grand tapestry, our hearts entwine.
By chance we met, or so it seems,
Destiny crafted our shared dreams.

In joyful moments and trials we face,
Our kinship blossoms, time can't erase.
With every secret, every sigh,
We build this fortress, we learn to fly.

As stars align in the vast expanse,
Life writes our story, a fateful dance.
In every heartbeat, our echoes blend,
A kinship forged, that will never end.

So here's to the bond that fate has spun,
In life's wild journey, we've already won.
In every moment, together we find,
Kinship beyond coincidence, beautifully aligned.

## Harmonies of Affinity

In gardens where laughter sings,
We plant seeds of gentle grace,
Every heart a note that clings,
Together, we find our place.

Breezes whisper through the trees,
Echoes of a shared delight,
Softly dancing in the breeze,
Guiding us through day and night.

Colors blend in vivid hues,
Creating a tapestry bright,
In every moment we choose,
To cherish the bonds of light.

Melodies of trust resound,
In the chorus of our dreams,
In unity, we are bound,
Flowing like harmonious streams.

With every heartbeat aligned,
We forge a path side by side,
In this journey, intertwined,
Together, we shall abide.

## Cultivating Connections

In gardens rich with shared intent,
We sow the seeds of trust and care,
Each moment shared, a time well spent,
Nourishing bonds that we bear.

Hands united in the toil,
We dig through earth with hearts so bold,
In rich dark soil, our spirits coil,
Tales of kindness waiting to be told.

With laughter like the sun's warm glow,
We water dreams with gentle hands,
In this safe space, love will grow,
As we nurture our sacred plans.

Through storms and trials, we stand tall,
Bearing weight with strength combined,
In every challenge, we can't fall,
For in each other, peace we find.

When roots entangle, deep and wide,
We find the strength to face the night,
In every heart, a place to guide,
Together, we ignite the light.

## Allies in the Journey


On winding paths, we walk as one,
Side by side through thick and thin,
In every challenge, we have fun,
With hearts entwined, we shall begin.

With shared burdens, we are strong,
In laughter's echo, joy does bloom,
Each tale we share, a vibrant song,
Filling up the empty room.

Through every storm, we weather well,
As allies forged in trust and grace,
With courage found, our spirits swell,
In this embrace, our rightful place.

With footprints marked in love's warm sand,
We venture forth, our spirits high,
No road too harsh, no dream too grand,
Together, we'll reach for the sky.

As stars align, we make our way,
With hope ignited by shared light,
In every dawn, a bright new day,
United, we'll conquer the night.

## Fellowship of the Chosen

In sacred circles, bonds ignite,
With trust as our guiding flame,
Each voice a star, so bold and bright,
Together we rise, none the same.

Through trials faced, we find our strength,
In whispered dreams that softly flow,
We journey forward, go the length,
With hearts aligned, we bravely grow.

With laughter sweet as morning dew,
We lift each other's weary soul,
In hands outstretched, we craft the view,
Creating a world, beautifully whole.

In silence shared, solace finds place,
With every tear, we shed the weight,
In this embrace, a warm embrace,
Fellowship, our shared fate.

Through every season, we will stand,
With hope woven in the threads,
A chosen bond, forever planned,
In love's embrace, our spirits wed.

## The Heart's Chosen Path

In whispers soft, the heart does steer,
A journey unfolds, casting out fear.
With every step on this sacred ground,
A melody sweet in silence is found.

Through valleys deep, the shadows play,
Illuminated by the dawn's first ray.
With courage held, the spirit ascends,
The path ahead where true love blends.

Each choice a mirror, truth reflects,
In the embrace of what connects.
A dance of fate, spun in the night,
Guided gently by starlit light.

Awakening dreams, the soul aligns,
Surrendered hopes on sacred lines.
With every heartbeat, the journey swells,
In the echo, a story dwells.

So trust the rhythm, let it unfold,
For the heart's chosen path is pure gold.
As seasons change, and moments flow,
In love's embrace, we freely grow.

## Followers of the Light

In shadows thick, we seek the glow,
A beacon bright where lost souls go.
Together we rise, united and bold,
As followers of light, our hearts unfold.

Through winding paths and darkest nights,
We find our way with whispered sights.
In every spark, a story long,
We lift each other, we grow strong.

With open arms, we gather near,
To share our hopes and cast out fear.
In laughter shared, a warmth we find,
As followers of light, our spirits bind.

The journey calls, we take the leap,
In shared devotion, our souls we keep.
With every step, we leave a trace,
Of love and kindness in this space.

So let us walk, hand in hand side by side,
In the glow of love, we shall abide.
For followers of light will always stand,
Together we rise, a glorious band.

## Serendipity in Souls

In chance encounters, destinies weave,
A tapestry rich, in hearts we believe.
With every glance, a spark ignites,
In the dance of fate, our love unites.

Through winding roads and whispered dreams,
Life's sweet serendipity gently beams.
With open hearts, we greet the day,
Finding magic in the ordinary's sway.

Together we laugh; together we sigh,
In moments shared, we learn to fly.
In serendipity, our souls collide,
In the currents of joy, we choose to ride.

Through storms and suns, we navigate,
In every heartbeat, love's gentle fate.
Reminded always to cherish the small,
For serendipity dances through it all.

So let us embrace what life unfolds,
In sweet surprises, our story molds.
In every turn, and every goal,
We find the beauty in each other's soul.

## **Handpicked Hearts**

In stillness found, our hearts entwine,
Two souls selected, a love divine.
Each heartbeat echoes what we choose,
Handpicked hearts, in joy we fuse.

With gentle whispers, the world stands still,
In shared glances, a love to fulfill.
Through every trial, side by side,
Handpicked hearts with nothing to hide.

In laughter shared, the burdens lighten,
A bond so strong that will not frighten.
Together we rise, as seasons change,
In handpicked hearts, love will arrange.

With every challenge, we dance and twirl,
In unified rhythms, our dreams unfurl.
A sanctuary built in sacred space,
Handpicked hearts, in love's embrace.

So here's to the pact of souls aligned,
In this journey, our fate defined.
For handpicked hearts will always soar,
Together we thrive, forevermore.

## Embracing the Circle

In the heart of the woods, we gather,
Leaves whispering secrets, full of grace.
Together we stand, hand in hand,
Creating a bond, a sacred space.

Circles of laughter, joy unconfined,
With each shared story, spirits entwine.
The moon casts shadows, soft and bright,
A tapestry woven in the night.

Nature wraps close, a warm embrace,
Each breath a promise, a gentle trace.
In this sacred space, we find our way,
As the stars above begin their ballet.

Together we rise, like the morning sun,
Uniting our hearts, as one we run.
In the dance of life, we find our role,
Embracing the circle, the wholeness of soul.

Fragile yet strong, like the roots of a tree,
Grounded in love, forever we'll be.
As seasons change and years unfold,
The circle remains, a tale retold.

## Handpicked Souls

In the quiet moments, we find our kind,
Gathered like flowers, handpicked souls unwind.
Each petal a story, each hue an embrace,
Together we bloom in this sacred space.

Through laughter and tears, our seeds have grown,
Under the sun, the love we have sown.
With roots intertwined, we stand so tall,
In the garden of life, there's room for us all.

Tales of the journey, we share by the fire,
Flickering flames igniting desire.
The warmth of connection, a shared heartbeat,
Echoes of friendship, life's sweetest treat.

Through storms and sunshine, side by side,
In the tapestry of life, we will abide.
Handpicked and cherished, our spirits align,
In this beautiful dance, your heart like mine.

So here's to the moments that weave us as one,
In the story of life, let our love be spun.
Handpicked souls gather, forever entwined,
In this garden of dreams, our hearts unconfined.

## The Fellowship of Echoes

In the valley deep where the echoes play,
Voices blend soft, like the break of day.
Together we wander, paths intertwined,
In harmony's cradle, our hearts aligned.

From mountains high to rivers flowing,
The fellowship whispers, ever growing.
Each echo a lesson, each sound a friend,
In the dance of the moment, we find our blend.

Through valleys of sorrow, the peaks of glee,
We walk hand in hand, in unity.
Together we rise, together we fall,
In the fellowship of echoes, we hear the call.

So let us remember, through thick and thin,
The strength of our voices, the warmth from within.
For in every echo, a story resides,
In the fellowship of echoes, where love abides.

As the sun sets low, casting shadows wide,
In the stillness, our spirits confide.
A bond unbroken, a journey of trust,
In the fellowship of echoes, we find what's just.

## Ties of Intent

In every heartbeat, a purpose stirs,
Ties of intent, woven with words.
With every intention, a thread we spin,
Creating a tapestry, life's divine grin.

Through choices made and paths we've crossed,
In the web of our lives, nothing's lost.
Each bond a connection, profound and true,
In the tapestry of time, they shine through.

In moments of stillness, we find our way,
With ties of intent, we seldom sway.
For every action, a ripple will send,
In the ocean of life, we bend and blend.

Though storms may rage and shadows loom,
In the ties of intent, we find our bloom.
Connected in spirit, we rise and soar,
In this journey together, we explore.

So let us remember, in every endeavor,
The ties we create are bonds forever.
With love as our compass and hope as our guide,
In the ties of intent, we'll always abide.

## The Family We Build

In laughter and in tears, we stand,
Together, side by side, hand in hand.
Through storms and sunshine, our roots grow deep,
In this loving bond, we find our keep.

With stories shared and memories bright,
We gather close in the warm twilight.
Every heart a thread, woven tight,
Creating a tapestry of pure delight.

Through trials faced, we rise anew,
In every moment, our love shines through.
We forge a home, a sacred space,
In the warmth of family, we embrace.

Each smile a beacon, each hug a shield,
In strength and kindness, we are healed.
With open arms and dreams to share,
In the family we build, we find our care.

No ties of blood could bind us more,
For love's the anchor we all restore.
In every heartbeat, we find our song,
Together forever, where we belong.

## Hearts Aligned in Destiny

Two paths converged on a starry night,
A whisper of fate, a spark of light.
With souls entwined, we dance as one,
Under the gaze of a rising sun.

In dreams we share, our hopes align,
In every heartbeat, your hand in mine.
Through every trial, forever strong,
Together we write our timeless song.

The universe pulls with a gentle grace,
Leading us onward, we find our place.
With hearts ablaze, we chase the dawn,
In the tapestry of love, we are drawn.

Moments fleeting, yet time stands still,
In your embrace, I find my will.
With every smile, the world is right,
In this sacred bond, our spirits ignite.

Destiny's thread weaves us near,
In every whisper, your voice I hear.
Together we rise, through thick and thin,
Bound by fate, our journey begins.

## Journeys Taken Hand in Hand

With every step, our story unfolds,
In laughter and whispers, our journey molds.
Through winding paths and skies of blue,
Hand in hand, we wander true.

Each mile a treasure, each view divine,
In shared adventures, our spirits align.
With courage and grace, we traverse the land,
In the beauty of moments, together we stand.

Through valleys low and mountains high,
With hearts as compasses, we reach for the sky.
In every heartbeat, a shared refrain,
In joy and struggle, love will remain.

As seasons change and time moves on,
The bond we cherish will never be gone.
With every sunrise, a promise anew,
Journeys taken, just me and you.

Together we write this epic tale,
With dreams as our sails, we shall not fail.
In the depths of our hearts, a map so grand,
For every journey is better hand in hand.

## **Bonded Through Purpose**

In the quiet moments, our purpose shines,
A mission aligned in sacred designs.
With hearts set ablaze, we rise each day,
Bonded through purpose, come what may.

Through trials faced, we find our way,
With every challenge, stronger we sway.
In unity's strength, we stand as one,
For the work we do is never done.

With passion ignited, we fuel the fire,
In every endeavor, we reach higher.
Together our dreams paint the sky,
In the art of living, we shall not shy.

With hands held steady, we craft our fate,
Each step forward, we celebrate.
In the heart of struggle, we find the goal,
Bound by our purpose, we are whole.

Through storms we navigate, side by side,
In the beauty of purpose, we take pride.
With every heartbeat, our vision clear,
Bonded through purpose, we persevere.

## The Fellowship of the Bold

In shadowed woods where dreams take flight,
A band of hearts in the starlit night.
They share their laughter, fears, and plans,
Together they rise, united they stand.

Through trials faced and battles fought,
With lessons learned and wisdom sought.
Hand in hand, they face the storm,
In every moment, their spirits warm.

The whispers of courage echo clear,
In the bonds of friendship, they hold dear.
With every step, the world they mold,
In the heart of night, they are bold.

From distant lands, their stories weave,
A tapestry of dreams to believe.
In laughter and tears, their spirits blend,
A fellowship strong that will not end.

Though paths may twist and times may change,
Their hearts remain in a dance, so strange.
Together they fight, together they soar,
The fellowship of the bold, forever more.

## **Threads that Bind**

In silent whispers, the threads they weave,
Connections made, what we believe.
Through joy and sorrow, laughter and pain,
The ties we forge in sunshine and rain.

With every heartbeat, a story spun,
Bound by the light of the setting sun.
From kindred spirits, love will arise,
In the dance of life, under endless skies.

Each thread a path, a journey, a song,
In the tapestry of time, they belong.
Together they shimmer, a vibrant hue,
The threads that bind, a bond so true.

When shadows creep, and doubts entwine,
These threads of trust, a lifeline divine.
Through every struggle, hand in hand,
We weave a future, together we stand.

In moments fleeting, in time's embrace,
The threads that bind us, a sacred space.
In unity's strength, the world we find,
A testament of love, forever entwined.

## Kin in the Cosmos

Across the stars, where the galaxies glow,
We search for kin in the cosmic flow.
In the depths of night, we reach for light,
Bound by the dreams of infinite sight.

Through time and space, our spirits dance,
In a universe vast, we seize the chance.
With every pulse, we share a song,
In this celestial world, we all belong.

From distant moons to suns that blaze,
We find connections in unseen ways.
In the heart of stardust, echoes reside,
Kin in the cosmos, forever our guide.

Through darkness deep, we carry a spark,
In the constellations, we leave our mark.
With open hearts, we seek and roam,
In the great expanse, we find our home.

With every heartbeat, the universe sings,
In the dance of eternity, hope takes wings.
Together we soar, together we dream,
Kin in the cosmos, a brilliant beam.

## The Bonds We Forge

Through trials faced and mountains climbed,
The bonds we forge are truly divine.
In the warmth of trust, we find our way,
Together we shine, come what may.

With each shared moment, a bridge we build,
In the garden of friendship, our hearts are filled.
Through laughter and tears, we find our grace,
The bonds we forge, time can't erase.

In shadows cast by fears unknown,
The light of kinship brightly shone.
With every step, we share the load,
In the dance of life, love is bestowed.

Through storms that rage and skies that clear,
The bonds we forge draw us near.
In silent strength, we find our voice,
Together in unity, we rejoice.

Though paths may twist and fates may turn,
In the hearts we hold, our passions burn.
The bonds we forge, a flame so bright,
In every struggle, we find our light.

## **Echoes of Intent**

Whispers of dreams in the night,
Calling the brave to take flight.
Intentions woven with care,
Breathe in the promise of air.

Footsteps trace a silent path,
Guided by fate, not by wrath.
Echoes ring through the quiet,
Resounding hope, hearts in riot.

Stars become symbols we trust,
In every shadow, our lust.
Intent leads us through the maze,
Illuminating the haze.

Connections drawn from the void,
Unspoken bonds, never toyed.
Dreams tread softly on this ground,
In each heartbeat, truth is found.

The night fades as we align,
Collective visions intertwine.
Echoes of intent shall stay,
Guiding us through light and gray.

## Embracing the Chosen Path

Steps unfold on destiny's weave,
Choices made with hearts that believe.
Trust the journey, let it flow,
In the unknown, seeds we sow.

Each twist and turn, a lesson learned,
In shadows deep, our spirits burned.
Through struggle, we shall arise,
Finding strength beneath the skies.

With every dawn, a fresh embrace,
New horizons, endless space.
Embrace the path that sings our name,
In joy and sorrow, still the same.

Together we stand, hand in hand,
United by dreams, vast and grand.
In every heartbeat, we persist,
Embracing what fate has kissed.

A journey painted with our vision,
Steps towards love, a bold decision.
Embracing the chosen path we tread,
With each heartbeat, we forge ahead.

## Brotherhood in a World Apart

Across the miles, our spirits meet,
In laughter, love, and stories sweet.
Brotherhood forged by the fire,
A bond that lifts, takes us higher.

Though distance stretches, hearts remain,
Through joyful moments and the pain.
Unified by dreams we hold,
Together, our destinies unfold.

The world may try to pull us far,
Yet in our hearts, we know who we are.
In silent support, we rise,
Finding strength in each other's eyes.

When shadows loom, we share the light,
Holding each other through the night.
In every challenge, we grow strong,
Together in spirit, we belong.

Brotherhood blooms in the dark,
A flame ignited, a steadfast spark.
No matter how far we may roam,
In each other's hearts, we find home.

## Synchronized Hearts

In the rhythm of life, we sway,
Hearts beating in a gentle play.
Each pulse whispers tales in time,
Together, we craft our rhyme.

Through the chaos, we find our song,
Melodies sweet, where we belong.
With every glance, our spirits bind,
In synchronized love, warmth defined.

Moments shared beneath the stars,
No distance felt, no lingering scars.
Every heartbeat, a sacred call,
In the dance of life, we stand tall.

When shadows gather, hope shines bright,
Guiding us softly through the night.
Linked together, we embrace,
A journey marked by love's grace.

Synchronized hearts, forever true,
With every beat, we make it through.
Hand in hand, our spirits soar,
In love's embrace, forevermore.

## The Bridge of Belonging

Across the river wide, we meet,
In laughter, life's rhythm, we find our beat.
Hands entwined, we walk the path,
Every step shared, creates our half.

Beneath the stars, we share our dreams,
Woven together, brighter it seems.
Each heartbeat echoes, stories unfold,
In this bridge of belonging, we are whole.

Seasons shift, but we stand firm,
In every twist, our hearts still warm.
Through storms and sunshine, we shall sway,
The bridge we built, will not decay.

With every whisper, a bond anew,
In silence, love's language speaks true.
Together we rise, our spirits soar,
United by trust, forevermore.

In this sacred space, we find our grace,
In the bridge of belonging, we've found our place.
Side by side, we greet the dawn,
A tapestry of love, we've drawn.

## Connected Souls

Two paths converge, where hearts align,
In quiet moments, all feels divine.
Through glances shared, and smiles wide,
Bound by a thread, we choose to bide.

In the rhythm of laughter, we dance,
Every glance a hopeful chance.
Together we weave through every trial,
Connected souls, we walk each mile.

With every sunset, bond grows strong,
In woven silence, we belong.
In shared burdens, we find our light,
Connected by dreams, we take flight.

After the storms, our roots entwined,
In the garden of love, we find.
With every heartbeat, our stories merge,
Connected souls, a constant surge.

In this tapestry, two become one,
Together we savor, the warmth of the sun.
Through the journey, hand in hand we go,
In this bond of love, we endlessly grow.

## Radiance of Intention

In the dawning light, our hopes ignite,
Each intention shines, so pure, so bright.
With every word, we pave the way,
In love's embrace, we shall not sway.

The whispers of morning call us near,
In the quiet moments, dreams appear.
Radiance glows in hearts aligned,
Guided by love, our futures bind.

With every action, a spark we send,
Creating ripples, we gently bend.
Together we rise, through shadows we roam,
In the radiance of intention, we find our home.

In the stillness, we cultivate grace,
Every step forward, a gentle trace.
Through the trials, our spirits soar,
In the radiance of love, we explore.

As the world unfolds, we take a stand,
With hearts united, we'll make our brand.
In intention's glow, we find our way,
In this dance of life, we shall stay.

## The Language of Togetherness

In each heartbeat, a word transcends,
In silence spoken, love never ends.
Through every glance, a story told,
In the language of togetherness, bold.

With gentle gestures, we weave a thread,
In the tapestry of life, love is spread.
In every smile, our spirits blend,
Bound by the ties that will not bend.

Across distances, we bridge the gap,
In this journey, we lay our map.
Through every challenge, hand in hand,
The language of togetherness, we understand.

In the laughter shared, we find our tune,
Beneath the stars, we dance by the moon.
Together we rise, in unity's glow,
In this language of love, we grow.

In every moment, connection thrives,
The language of togetherness, it drives.
In each heartbeat, we'll always find,
In love's embrace, our souls aligned.

Printed in the USA
CPSIA information can be obtained
at www.ICGtesting.com
CBHW070345041224
18174CB00083B/76